From The Word Go

MURRAY EDMOND

AUCKLAND UNIVERSITY PRESS

For Harriet

First published 1992
Auckland University Press
University of Auckland
Private Bag 92019, Auckland

ISBN 1 86940 067 4

Publication is assisted by the Literature Programme of the Queen Elizabeth II Arts Council

Typeset by Deadline Typesetting Limited
Printed by University Printing Services

Distributed outside New Zealand
by Oxford University Press

But you remember how it was. You touched the word, or perhaps it touched you, and it was released, or it was you who were released, so that about that time things began. You spoke about things you did not understand, it was pleasurable, the returning again and again to the paper. You possessed, or were possessed by, the sense you had discovered. *What* did not matter to you. That was a long time ago now. In the beginning there was the going on. Later you advanced by a series of stoppages. You tried not to reduce the world to the simple intentionalities of poems. You lived in language and found it like walking out deeper and deeper into water. When it was up to your nipples you could not see your cold toes. You imagined them. You extended yourself. You escaped the knowingness language was made up of arbitrary signs. How small they were, how sharp, how ongoingly amusing in the way they could bring you up short. As in cold water splashed between dry shoulderblades. Contraction of muscles at base of follicles, erection of papillae. That much at least you were able to find out later. Up they go. The word go. Its presence. Off you go now.

By the same author

Entering the Eye (1973)
Patchwork (1978)
End Wall (1981)
Letters and Paragraphs (1987)
(edited with Mary Paul) *The New Poets* (1987)

Contents

Acknowledgements

Untold
NZ Listener
Sport
Landfall
Magnum Bonum

'Hirsute Canine Narrative' was first printed in a pamphlet by Auckland University Press.

The Word Go

Go.
You begin
by imagining yourself
that theatrical act
at a window
the flat sea
stretching from the Corniche
and hungry penniless barefoot
prostitute boys
going about like yachts
all that wartime glam
and a short bespectacled man
in khakis and lemon-squeezer
beside his YMCA truck.
Febrile heat makes
ghosts —
towards him
across the Mediterranean
comes a small blond boy
walking on water
clutching a typewriter.
Go.
And you go.
Now.
And it's now.

Dead Lines

shoot that tui off its tree

in the bay where the dead sheep lay one day

separating the boys from the buoys

signs taken for tokens wonders sold as toxins

tinniness tinnitus tocsins tininess

words bottled in books

history debrided of stories hisses alone

prey prey prey on your mind for a prayer

knowing only the knowing of no no no no no no

25/1/91

The Life Frieze

When I placed them together they acquired all at once a ring they never possessed individually — just as if they could not be exhibited with others. And so I put them together in friezes.
— Edvard Munch

Faviola

In the stories we tell about the stories we told
her eyes used to follow you round the room
but only if you didn't look at her directly.
She would listen in a way which was faint, romantic,
forward-leaning, mobile beneath her red cowl,
attentive to the micro-gradations of emotion
in the confessional *sotto voce* of the small boy.
How sick he always looked to her. But this was a very public
room, coming and going with lower case life in its
proliferating nullity, its small, tepid, intense handshake,
its grasp of the lunchtime musical, I'm just a girl
who cain't say no, poor Judd is dead, I almost
forgot the blue-eyed kid — all these she bent towards
giving me the velvet of her ear as a comfort.
How could one have sucked succour from what one
poured oneself into, the whorl of the skull's cave, the instantly
clanging cochlea of instantly being heard —
all the fights she saw, the naked children whipping
each other with towels, the fire leaping up to greet
their sadism, evening inundating them with its
sodium passion, nuclear splendour, poisonous, religious
cloud chamber, postwar elegance, the best of everything
in a nutshell. She was always there. Of course.
She was mother at rest among the curling apple peelings.
Her hand held his wet brow as he coughed into the basin.
She was several stories high.
He began suspecting things.
Mother of all nurses, matrix of the house.
Her presence amongst uncles was so taken for granted
it was unnoticed.

Bradman
(for Rod Edmond)

Even as the one great umpire was
writing against your name on a scale of one to ten, you were
rolling round on the bed beating the wall
doubled with the laughter of fiction while
he looked down on you, the paternal image, nothing
catholic, but a grand, protestant cricketer.
In your small room
green and brown without a hair out of place
nothing against your name but the sin of loneliness
locked in your cell from birth
and refusing to come out when released
for fear of losing the approbation of the great cricketer,
the gently raised and censoring finger —
it was a tale told of another age by boys
who were men at which you laughed with such fractious delight.
I'd like to re-run several instalments like
a radio serial, a hamper full of jokes, a summer full
of evenings listening for the last ball to be bowled.
Scorer, whittler, scrimshaver,
crouched with your spoon in the corner of your stone cell
(even as the commentary ran on year by year)
you scratched and scraped grain by grain
to grind an escape from the fearsome chateau.
Even your own spit was a corrosive on the stone.
Then, one midnight, breakthrough at last —
a gleam of water twinkles two hundred feet below
up through the breach you've dug in the granite flags,
your own innings over.
But where to go in this nowhere world of sea and endless wind
and spume drift spun in air?
A boy's own agony was what was writ in water against your name.
But then you spotted it —
a piece of rusted pipe to clamber down,
a clammy hank of salt-shredded rope to swing the gap,
a ledge on the sheer rock to inch along
with meagre foothold
and a tiny niche where you might eke out the night
with waiting while your doom crept closer.

And the wind howled.
But look!
Could that beetling shadow on the cliff presage rescue,
could there lurk a secret opening there? And, yes,
in fact the fabled passage to the lost treasure
has just fallen to your luck.
Remember the umpire's gaze is fixed, as in a picture.
There was always a blind spot in the room where his looking
could not reach.
As the stories told it, there was always a way out,
always, at five minutes to six, another day to play.

The 1895 Kiss

Was he dreaming of buying a hay paddock
in Okura for $1.1 million as he kissed her?
How did something so rigid with desire
get on the wall? Is it possible to compose
a narrative only of questions? Were the curtains
left open so that the neighbours across
the street in the apartment block and the men
in the warehouse and the uniformed women
at the industrial machines could watch them,
their warm, naked bodies buttoned together
at the lips? Did the neighbours whisper
to each other: 'Her blood-red hair has enveloped
him.'? Did the warehousemen murmur as their
afternoon shoulders brushed, exchanging
waybills, 'He has wound himself round her
like a blood-red snake.'? Did the women, coughing
towards the evening of the nineteenth century,
exclaim: 'She has sent a chilling lust through
his body, she has pressed her body violently
against his.'? Even if the sole intent of the two,
the woman and the man, had been to misdirect
the street, to stir the whole town up
with wave on wave of inexhaustible words pulsing
through its wires, did they themselves perhaps
feel themselves perhaps both moisten like soap
or eyes as the soft smell of each other's hair

as rich as fresh ink choked their nostrils, throats,
tongues, as her hand found his shoulder, blundered
into it like a moth in the dark and noted
its precocious life fluttering at her touch?
Did they not once walk together as light departed
over the hay paddock and feel the blank moths
implode like soft bullets on their separate skins?

The discovery she made about nature was that
everything in it has a name, every part and parcel
of it is distinguished from every other part
and parcel; and each parcel contains some means,
sexual or otherwise, of reproducing itself.
In the hay paddock, was she confronted by the huge fact
of her own ignorance and tempted to rename everything
in her own image once and just once
so each name should be forgotten as soon as
it was born?

As the child is the child of the child
of the child, the kiss is remembered for ever.
He set it in ink like a sentence in 1895.

Snake

Grey linoleum, grey formica, grey paint,
silver taps and cupboard handles, coupe louvres,
stainless steel bench, grey-blue table top,
white fridge, lemon walls, and swimming there,
my snake, how I wanted him there, on the wall,
my golden snake (the gold are venomous)
who came curling lazily out of a child's
reptilian grief of love withheld, mismanaged,
timed-to-perfection, and bent his head
(they must be killed) round the water pitcher
and lazily lifted his head and looked lazily
round him, while the mongoose danced and danced,
all the while lazily all the while with
enormous strength subduing his desire
to eat his own tail, to tangle with the alchemy
of the kitchen. He was mine. I painted him

myself, thick damp paint padded on wallpaper,
an ochre splodge unwinding formlessly through
poisonous Sicilian weeds and an overworked lattice
of broken bricks, the well itself, the place
to draw from. And I was waiting, as he waited
for the snake to drink, as I waited for the present
to go up on the wall and propitiate, initiate,
shamanise, the way certain words like leukaemia
or megaton, Reader's Digest or Gershwin's Rhapsody
in Blue could transpose a room.
In the nineteen fifties everything was made of gold —
the snakes were made of gold, the love was made of
gold, the kitchen taps ran gold from the burning bowels
of the earth and far-off Etna smoked gold smoke.
This was my painting of my snake, an archaeology
before the paint had even dried or cracked. Which
it did. An antique alive and well in its own time.
That Prince, another who missed his chance,
who wondered to our face if fardels should be borne
at all, had no hesitation heaping his well-to-do
emotional blackmail on Ophelia. What we saw,
as he spoke to us, was his self-hate, his self-scorn,
the snake of his hand reaching out to her
to withhold love.

The Blue Boy

What manner of child was this
who turned the heads in Milne and Choyce
at the quality of cloth he wore,
the fine bone china of his hand,

the way a cricket ball would roll
with linseed touch across his palm
and devilishly elude the batsman's
prod? The mothers all swooned

when he drew his dirk and foil
and danced at Christmas time
in the forecourt of the petrol station.
Fathers were not so taken

with his *jouissance.*
For one thing, growing up
wasn't on his purposeful agenda.
His body language told them something

they pretended not to want to hear.
And in space he hybridised
the Victorian and the Continental:
chasms vast of cliff and crag

floating in sublimity of storm and sea
were melded with the café corner,
enclave with absinthe and a dream.
He was the boy you were born to fall

in love with, the child every mother
ached to hang upon her wall.
He drove that kind of 1930s sportscar,
had a library of erotica,

smelt as other men then did not smell
and got away with it
because his Dickensian offsider, the Red Boy,
took the rap.

That such a spiv as that Blue Boy
was living in the lounge, a room
parlous with dignity where you were taken
when the doctor came, a ripe needle
in a whack of buttock, standing on a chair

so the doctor didn't have to bend,
this was his enchantment.
From his rock settle he looked across
a tuneless piano to a glass flamingo.

Dutch Interior

When you came into the room there she was
plumb in a corner with her broad back
comfortably wedged into the panelling

and watched by a small, interior clutch of children.
It was quite quiet.
There was no sense of horror
as it is registered in a scream
or speechlessness.
Her suckling of the baby was bountiful,
loving even,
and the looks on the children's faces
(they were turned away but you could read them
from behind)
indicated incomprehension and curiosity
but also acceptance.
The pattern of the floor, green-black and grey-white squares
of marble, large and peacefully laid out,
and the calm light which streamed down through a high side
  window,
and all the restful, warm stillness
were totally reassuring.
You knew simply this couldn't be a place
where something inhuman would happen.
Not this light-filled corner of the bedroom
where the armless chair sat
jalousied by shadow cast by the venetian blinds
and the safe things like hand-mirrors and combs and brushes
and bibles and barometers were evenly spaced
on crocheted doilies on the polished rimu.
It was the kind of place you came and quietly sat between
the heavily skirted knees of your mother
while she sang an old French song
and sorted the headlice eggs from the strands of your hair.
You asked her to tell you about what she had done as a girl
before you were born
and before she met your father
and she cut and peeled you a piece of apple
and you took it
marvelling something could be so clean and crystalline,
so light and fleshy at the same time,
so sweet and yet make your eyes water when you bit it,
and when you glanced up for an instant
through the happy tears
your mother's face

was the face of a woman you had never seen before,
the lustre on the high dome of her forehead
was completely unfamiliar
and yet how could you not recognise her?
after all she was your mother.

Crows over a Cornfield

It spoke disaster on a grand scale.
The kids knew it was Freudian.
The folks did not.
Impasto crows aching with depth
and with excess
who made no attempt to scumble
the murder in their minds.

The way the joke was not got meant
a moral sampler may as well have hung:
An Englishman
Never Raises His Foot or If
You Can Keep Your
Head When All Around You someone or
other Is Losing Theirs

above the fireplace. But the kids chose
this, Who Suffers Wins or Misery Is
Truth. Oh artists,
radiant with defeat, the victim's ears
can be taken out
on loan. No other picture could have
quite so well subsumed

the family iconography. Since it was
the last thing you saluted,
car keys clutched
for dear dear life, before
you left the house.
From woe unto expunging woe like
Ishmael, afloat the coffin in the Classic

Comic wearing long pink combinations,
gazing out beyond the creamy pool
where the *Pequod*
sank, to sight the *Rachel*,
devious-cruising.
No other final frame ever caught so well
the sense of something coming up

when everything was coming to an end.
As if rounding a nothing-special bend
on the way to
the Ohaupo pub after hours
you caught a crow
in the foggy beams and thought,
'Now that reminds me of something or other.'

Reunion

By the time this poem reaches you it will be
Thursday, the day I ride the subway as the man
who never returns, a swan plant with a monarch
under one arm, a bowl of tadpoles and a sheaf
of potato cuts opposed. I'm never coming home.

She'll be laughing, missing the joke by a country
mile, but laughing, she'll be saying Shot himself?
some people will do anything to get themselves in
a song   and all the old faces will be ringing her
with folksy steps in cowboy suits and fairy gear

and one boy will have the whole carriage transfixed
as he mimes a woman *au toilette*, lipstick, handbag,
bra, the lot, the rest of us with faces busted up
like Picasso mezzotints fit to laugh or cry or gape
but aching at the calligraphic moment of trans-

figuration opening wide for the Murder House. His fate
is still unlearned though word has got around he's done
nicely for himself, has transplanted fullsize Phoenix
palms to his foreshore garden while many others never
left or peaked long before the divorce came through.

Rerun

Old Caesar Roose's barge
lies rotting on the tombolo . . .
and our childhood bogey, that bodgie,
the 'Banana Boy', the one at whom
we jeered then scarpered screaming
the day he rode his bike along
MacDiarmid Rd eating a banana . . .
Red-berried may in March
who guards the little dry culverts . . .
in motel land with golden-gravel paths
and silver dollar trees and gardens
soft as bark . . . a sky like porcelain
and vinyl creamed with blood completes
the damage . . . Jesus loves me, this
I know . . .

Ode to Virgil Exner

He had led Chrysler, the last stronghold of engineering and sanity in the industry, away from substance and into flash.
— Thomas Hine

Still weaving the body's ontogenetic narrative
and unravelling it each night
like the gym frock you took off, Lucy, and
put on in diurnal course ('the new shape of motion')
history decanted and recanted using merely
two bottles, never spilling a drop
(Did you ever see anything like that in the Lake District?)
and it's easier to open the doors of the heart
saying yes, yes, this is real
and to walk out into the storm of the mind
discarding borrowed style.   Toot!   Toot!
goes the image train
as it passes Poor Tom's A-Collier'd Station
just south of Tooting Fuck.

There were three puriri trees
and a body under each
and leeches in the swamp
(one had your name on, baby) ('Frenched headlights —
you could get five kids across the back seat')
and such sublime singing all afternoon in the hills
('E tika, nga reo o nga mate') — 'Marilyn Monroe
as a housewife' — and your orphan breasts
in silhouette through your blouse as the low sun
snapped you rising from a barbecue sea.
Jiving on the beach at night,
the tail fins etched into the moonlight,
her matador legs shuffle the sand,
cha cha cha-cha-cha.

We all got back too late that night
some with diarrhoea and some with allergies
and some who looked down into the plain brown murky
wrapper of the camp stream's glass

and saw nothing they recognised as theirs.
Your signature of superimposed boomerangs was on
everything.   'Suddenly it's 1960.'
The stylist on the spot decants your world.
Drowned Scottish sailors and disembodied patupaiarehe
singing. Murray, Murray, she were bonnie,
thou wert braw. Douglas came out of the bush
a centipede hanging like a scarab from his thumb.
Satisfactory pain glistened in his eyes.
The '57 model's like a Lucy now:
'no motion has she now, no force'.

Hamilton

frocks in shops
desire desire

profit and loss
la gioconda

gazebo pergola
lagan and dross

stop and cross
Parana pariah

dog on log on
water own lone

proper bone clean
no matter mother

kiri
kiri
roa

getting the tone
doing the ton

ficus and malus
    rower

in mid-stream
property of

and a car and a
shop called

La Gonda
gone under

SOS

Subtly orchestrated sounds arising out of past memory told him there was no way through now and he endeavoured to make her aware of his predicament — that he was lost — without slipping out sound and stepping carefully to avoid his weight snapping or cracking on the brittle stones and sharp, obdurate spoor of worms cast in dry castles where the path broke away at the edges, but there was nothing their feet could manage in the way of lightness or softness or deftness, no sleight of sole which stopped all the fallen twigs and leaves from this year and the last and the last cacophonating at the slightest forward motion, so dry was the place now, so empty of liquid, so full of light, where he had lain, as a child, as she had heard him say, where he had hidden himself to listen to the conversation on the lawn below, where, as she remembered him saying over and over again, he had heard the round black man in the wheelchair, a man as bald as a photograph on art paper with a blanket over his knee and huge, amorphous glasses slung in his tartan lap like binoculars, say, 'If he comes over here again, the sneaky squirt, I'll give him hell cats!' when there was no one in the garden to listen or acknowledge except the hidden boy stretched under the macrocarpa arms wriggling on his stomach, fit to bust with terrible laughter or laughable terror, caught even then in the reversals of language, the language of reversals, as she still knew him to be, pushing back one of the skeletal brown branches, silicate, ossified, saliferous vegetation with only a faint twinge of green, a small flame of moisture at the tip, this place leached of its nourishment and robbed too of its familiar signs, its landmarks of return so that whereas she had gone ahead pushing off to the left where the path had always petered out and where they, he, sometimes with others, had always (always in the then) made the dash, some miserable yards, ten, twelve, maybe fifteen in the winter when the deciduous trees had shed, before reaching the further cover of willows and tall grass and another longer drop down a bank into a pit of slime and mud and reeds with a small creek and its delicious hoard of eels and some rare crayfish, none of which he recognised because none of it was there at the most distant point, the point across the grass, and nor was the round bald black man there in his wheelchair, being dead, so she went on plunging or ducking or weaving herself like thread while he was behind her trying to reach her with warning, silence, opportunity, secrecy, but, not able to make sound, she did not turn, he could not reach her to make her because only he responded to the synaesthesia of past and present, the tick of the dry bottles of space, ominous, syncopated.

Cookbook

At Sunday School
I rose to read:
Sure to Rise.

Home Movies

Knusper, knusper, kneischen,
Wer knuspert an meinem Häuschen?
*
Der Wind, der Wind
Das himmlische Kind.
— Brothers Grimm, 'Hansel and Gretel'

HOME

[place where one
lives house family
or other group country
city birthplace residence
during one's early
years dear to one
environment habitat
where something is
invested founded developed
building organisation
to care for informal name
for mental hospital one's
own ground objective
towards which a player
strives area where a player
is safe from attack]

MOVIES

[sequence of images moving
objects optical illusion
of continuous movement
projected screen flexible
strip of emotion-coated
cellulose to make negative
and trans(parent) coat layer
sheet fine haze mist blur
gauzy web filaments
fine threads abnormal
opacity tissue pathé
logic diseases]

Travelogue 1958–59

At Boydtown, the whalepots, for boiling
                        little boys.
                        At the Sydney Cricket Ground
Neil Harvey plays across the line, at the MCG
Alan Davidson runs in. There was no snake
in the grass to film. Striped swim towels
on the burning vinyl car seats.
Elegant dark glasses, wide collar of
green print dress. Albatross above your head,
Mother, Hen and Chickens lying out behind.
I felt
the blood in my veins turn to water.
Knees weak with piracy. You loved
me more than I loved you.
You saw it on the film.
My eyepatch face alert with greed,
crossed bones, candy homes.
Don't get changed in the
changing sheds. Put your togs on before
you go. Striped warm towels on the burning
vinyl elegant glasses. Behind the whaling station
a small hill rises. Track. To go through
grass in this foreign land, take a stick.
Ward off albatrosses. Keep your back
foot firmly anchored as you climb.

Horror Movie

He's got a wristwatch.
The yew trees, tiny things then,
frame him as he consults it.
Birthday face in camera.
                        He's got a bike.
Straddles it.
                        He's got promise.
He's buried it at the bottom of
                        the garden.
                        A bone.
                        He's got a new T-shirt
and shorts on.

Front lawn stiff.
He's got a tartan rug
for making love. The hinges
swing without a squeak.
He's holding a giant burnt-orange
fly agaric
by its mortal stem.
He's moving in
to the candy house this very day.
The whole small cow-town's
come out
to see him in.
He's got a seat in the loony bin.
Once he's made a move like that
there's no going back.
Ho ho ho
ho. Oh, look,
home is the place you can't go
back to.
He's seen that one a score of
times. Never fails to scare him silly.
Never fails to please.
You aim too please.

Good Black Friday, 1990

Cult Classic

dreaming of . . . love — Samuel Beckett, *Come and Go.*

1

50 feet of white light. Out of fog, a log. On the river, afloat. And who are those ones — angels? Girl in white and blue cotton dress, small boy scrambling (like a dog) on hands and feet, the sandy bank under his paws, slip-sliding away. And that place, the tree, the small seat, invisible except for the shape of people sitting, the rope swing, conic heaps of sand, where is that place? Some place. Some place which cannot be brought back. And the dog — Jack? Sam? Mutt? Mutt the mutt? — yes, one very place. But gone. Buried. A bone, buried. A single place. Alone. But gone.

She watches the boy. Who watches the dog. Who watches the girl. Action. Pared back. Bare. Packed. Close to not doing. An acrobat's stillness. Acceptance of the weight. Weightless in space, yet falling. Falling, yet waiting.

Jack the dog gets lost in the fog. The boy goes after the dog. The log goes out of sight. All swallowed in the white light. Bones. Gone. Alone. God, she sits, by god, on a broad tree-trunk lying on air out over the river. Her hair white and her skin white, the white light white with lightness. She rests, pale dress limp on knees. A saltimbanque needing nothing. The eyes rise to watch. Eyes of many, many. Many like fish. Piranha. Parana. Many many. Like coins. The river flows below her, that carpet on which the guilty munificience of happiness has showered coins of light. White faces. Meniscus broken by eels. Wings shadow water. The rings. And again.

2

At home, she waits, blinds down, door locked, the rooms' gloom slaked by jalousies of light. Venetian slashes. She stalks the dark, inside, checking locks, stops, clocks her feet, ticking, tick tock, tick tock. And they go, thid thud, they stop. She won't let them in. Won't. The children come but are not seen. The husband comes, but is not seen. Voices come and go. They leak in, in cracks, in the dark, through chinks in the skin of the house. The house goes, *thrim thrim*. It hogs her, dogs her, its feet follows her. In there. She still.

3

The park. God grant not. On the log. Oh. Dark. So. As little visible as possible. The sitting. The rings. No rings. The one. But only one. Not the two. Not the three. To flow. To vie. To rue. A life. One. Not there.

Road Movie Canto
(for Marion Edmond)

steel string
fiddle whine
focus homing in
battered suitcase lift-the-lid
shoebox, Skellerup, tarred with dust
'those ol' rolls
of celluloooooid . . .'
rerun harmonic line

who wanted to write about
Doris Lessing
raise a dozen kids
marry a poet who couldn't make up his mind
disappearance and reappearance

forget that:
out to watch the queens mime, night after night
'Ah got ma moooojo . . .'
purr of male throats
sandpaper birds
scrambling drinks
and cigarette machines, coming
home to read Frank O'Hara
'foolish enough to find it in wind . . .
'lyrical to a fault . . .
'in the terrible Western world . . .
'could not change it into history . . .'

Rangatihi upoko i takaia ki te akatea
on the bushline of Pirongia
learning the whakatauki,
Karioi away to north and west
over the Raglan Road
winding down the deviation
battered suitcases falling left and right
'gentle lovin' people . . .'

leg torn away from leg
piece out of piece unpieced
riding the ambulance
slow slow slow, oh, 15 mph
to curb the judder
    cushion pain
    stars

starry white flowers
notched in a crux of felled stump
    iron wood
    womb matrix
    winded wind
    heartwood
    white-flowered
    vine, creeper
        clear
hot-wired, trailed, shot-at, pursued possee-ed
    some lonesome Bonny or Clyde in honey-filter
to come at last to cottonwoods
at sundown
pick triggering strings like a hail of fire
from the sheriff's hidden men,
alive with fancy hats, beret
trilby cloth cap high felt hippy hat
'49 Wolseley, riding the running board,
champagne draughts from gallon stein

    body torn open
scattered and replaced
    head rebound with myrtle

Melodrama

In the grass beside the hydrangeas
a sign reading A GHOST.

The husband's taking tea with
his wife upon the lawn.

She looks stern: their daughter
drifts in white and blurrs.

The villain enters on a trike.
His silent eloquence is thin and loud

with gestures of conquest.
The hero draped in hat and cloak

ruptures the hydrangeas on the right.
He's arrived at last:

THE CHASE. Bodies fall
on bodies but the villain gets away.

Like a virus that mutates he
squirms to fight another day.

The husband teaches drama, his wife
owns a café in New York,

their daughter teaches music.
The hero's a lawyer, sends his sons

to Kings. The villain's lost
in Spain. A GHOST.

The Space of Time

(for Michele Leggott)

in which
it takes to grow
must be like
what it must have been like
to go
(oh
so
slow
by boat to Cathay
say
like waiting for a launch
to come and take you to
oh
you know
like opening a book no
like opening a packet (slow slow boat
and finding inside
the longed-for surprise and say
it's okay
like language can only
be made as simple
as language can be made:
'Tickets please!
All aboard!
Cast off!' —
Pool, Pole and Poot, local
demographers, predict
a baby boom that will
down the track aways conflict
with the pursuit of happiness
'integrational dependency squeeze'
but
'right now none of this is going to spoil
anyone's
fun'.
We are assured. Reassured. We wait.
What arrives will always be ready-made
at hand a coast looming a cry
like this?
'Land ahoy!'

Hirsute Canine Narrative

(for Kendrick Smithyman)

. . . men have always lounged in myths
as Tall Stories.
— W. H. Auden, 'Archaeology'

Auden, so you said, sought out the church where
the language was the least intelligible.
(It isn't known if he stopped you with stories
of penguins *en route* from LA
to New York.) An office next to yours means
you learn 'a thing or two'. So, entering in,
knowing no one, unable to speak to
any, he found there what was most form, most

spoke itself yet was unbetrayed. (Penguins
advancing in a line, up the freeway.)
Form, if you like, the measure of the writing
on, the transformation, substantiation,
in a time and place, to function. He sought
the moment of anachronism, the
trowel's crisp cut through crust, the lost city
full of holograph. Just as ivory

the knife handle is, head of seed as coat
is or shirt that's worn as worm, the pale ooze
of shoes from tree, drip drip drip, or penguin,
stuffed of course, raising his glass, from side of
mouth, 'Darling, when can we leave?' strangled by
his tie and tux. (What was that punchline now?
One hundred and twenty-nine penguins to
deliver — and the truck broke down way out west

on an endless shoulder of the seal, sun
ripe to dehydrate — up drives a rescue.)
Nature is transformed to recognition,
made unintelligible, becomes a rite,
when turned to story, what used to be called
his story. Someone spotted Auden, a

year before he died, hardsucked peachstone
instead of face, on the Cornmarket, Oxford,

looking for a corner to turn, the act
over and above the destination,
crossing and recrossing familiar ground,
as in Escher, each time on a higher
and higher level. ('Where're you taking those
penguins?' 'To the Bronx Zoo, they're gonna die
if I don't —' 'Let me help.' 'Sure am beholden —'
'Don't mention it —') 'History being made'

he wrote, 'by the criminal in us'. So,
raconteur of jokes, whose hand leaves quietly
a new poem waiting on the desk when I
come back from lunch, owner of that eyebrow
circumflexing irony while passing
down the corridor, how many crimes? Who
set up goodness versus history,
the song against the story, the choice of

archaeology or rite, teaching
over doing — those terms you twiddle like
a set of dials while sliding, slipping,
into the slide and unable to stop,
on a dune's weather side near Tomarata,
wind and sand in teeth and hair, a rite of
passage downwards — your foot disturbs — what?
Is this the archaeologist at play

or a serious penguin performing
ritual somersaults of animistic
obeisance? In the theatre of your words
the rite of poem-making is allowed
the same excuse to live as the long-lost
fact, the denotation of wind-buried past
in '. . . pieces of fossilized gum . . . moa crop . . .
of jasper . . . oven stones . . . shale spills . . . middens . . .'

Truck fixed, he set out east chasing penguins.
Driving into the Big Apple, there they

were, all one hundred twenty-nine of them,
waddling through the underpass. The traffic
is banked up behind. He calls out: 'Can't you
find the zoo?' And the reply: 'We've been to
the zoo — I had some money left — they want to see
Coney Island.' And did they get there,

like ratings on parade along the ferry
rail, priestly flippers extended toward the
big dipper's Möbius silhouette? The joke
does not tell. Lucky the man (Auden's words)
who can't prove much of what he says. More fun
that way. When one story ends begin an-
other. More fun that way, your way. And so,
the poem must end — and so it does!

Holiday

my body like any
body's body
diving naked in
deep water

*

Sophocles'
withdrawing
sigh, you roll
over

*

        each of us
lay down, spread-
eagled, each drew
round the other an out-
line:

'How small—'
'I can't be that size—'
'There must be more to me
than that—'

*

Monopoly.
Night swim.
Street lamp's glass bowl
a black mass
of insect bodies.

In bed, beside you,
warm, wanting to
go back and dive in.

*

Eternal note of
sadness. Have
you got Mr Flower
the Baker? Sorry,

not at home. Are
you visiting? Are you
enjoying your stay?
Isn't it a lovely day.

Enjoy your French sticks.

Pnigos

laughter of old texts/breathless,
                    the way to the god/through
his stomach, here on this island
                    paradise fierce children at
dawn roar for milk/no way of
                    denying their polymorphality/laughter
of old trees/low-flying plagues
                    infest the water supply and demand/
solidus of light which marks the day//
                    to read to feed . . .

yarrow/Queen Anne's lace, culvert/
                    ditch, beauty parlour/hairdresser,
agapanthus, paspalum, plantain, Jeyes
                    Fluid, taraire, tawapou, karamu,
hoon/lout/yobo, peacock, phoenix, tacky
                    cause and effect, 'nother cracker berry
hits the roof/3 a.m. monkey's paw kn-kn-knocking
                    every time this happens the fridge
switches off or on . . .

into the same bed no man slips twice/
                    how did we come? by boat
at midday, pies/ice creams/local features,
                    don't waste your wishes/one
pleasure for men for women one/paradise
                    a storm blown off course/in your house
afternoon no blinds light across ankles
                    tongue to toe alive with lying love unloops
legs of breathless . . .

laughter moonlight streetlight mosquito
                    cloud beachnight hightide
pebble-eyed/arise too far knees
                    splash bodies shed midnight/
milk/elbow and bloodeye caught/
                    the god has come to dismember you
with laughter/whether the best

verses sink the scales like swimmers
plunge or soar the air seagull style/spectacle
accumulated capital of desire . . .

Cool in versions

speak of the body's traps
reach down and touch there
below the belt
cerebellum territory
we fight ourselves
like a ship on a distant shore
all guilt and images
a paste of trade
songs without example
newspaper bleeding isobars
over Tasman's nowhere sea
redeemed by you invitation
travel the field of water
knocking like a shell
in wind
the bone ear
tongue luck
tune

Go to Woe

I'm glad I found you.
I thought we should talk.
I believed you would understand.
I didn't know what I was letting myself in for.
Not that it wasn't fun. Are you kidding!
Not that some things couldn't have been different.
The bed was too narrow.
The house was too quiet.
The time was too short.
I admire your honesty.
I think it's impossible.
I meant it as a friendly gesture.
I don't know. Sometimes. Why. You have that look.
In your eye.
Even if I knew now what I didn't know then I still don't know
  if I'd—
I never felt you were hiding anything.
Did you take a bath afterwards?
This was what I saw when I asked myself what the future would
  be.
Now I'm here.
I'm touched.
Touched?
Touched . . .
It's the way it goes on, went on . . .
Did you plan it, I mean, when you rang did you?
You were excited, you wanted.
I was scared, I wanted.
The soap. The soap felt. I touched. The soap. The soap.
And the soap felt.
The soap smelt.
The soap melt.
I want to know why why keep it up for so long.
Why is one experience so different from another.
Why is something like this important.
You can't be specific.
Grave and specific.

I think you are very warm. Warm and soft. Warm and soft and
sensitive.
I feel you are hiding a lot.
For instance, physically, weren't you tired?
You felt better and better as the summer wore on.
You wore less and less.
And grew more and more desperate.
So you said nothing.
Nothing.
What did you do when you came to part?
What did you say? What did you dance?
I can't say. You can't say.
Free.
Free.
Didn't you say free?
No. Not me.
I thought.
By free you mean alone.
Alone.
Alone and in love.
In love and walking.
Walking and stopping to look in the shop windows.
Watching yourself.
The books, the brandy, the clouds moving past the curtain.
The night moon catching their silver bellies.
There was no moon.

How to Write Laments

There was one who had grown more and more able
to believe in the failure
of hope as she grew older,

there was one who would applaud at the slightest
provocation even when the actors
would rather she didn't

there was one who sang in clubs at night
and answered the telephone by day
who gazed at her feet

one who was remembered for her performance as
a Russian wife, Saturday afternoon
theatre at Lyall Bay, an occasion

another whose father had a reputation which is
now spoken of as though it
was past, an author, a mother

one had a blind father, never seen by us
but included as part of
the struggle, an origin, to be known about

one, photographer, contortionist, acrobat
verité, in truth as shy as and
as sweet as, oh who shall supply

the words? others, not there, were dead; or
'away'; even forgotten; anger, pain,
nostalgia, silent in profusion

amongst? between? inside? 'those dreadful
acoustics'; how they fluttered like
anxious sparrows, mimetic hands, conversations

dense with music, enclaves of late-night
eyes by neon pulses
and they danced together in a crocodile

on the stage, down the steps and into the aisle
trying to escape
while the singing made splendid

the faces of those who once
found 'the transformation of society'
a normal excuse for assembly.

Dérive à la Frank
(for Fee Day)

25/7/66–25/7/89
23 years to the day.
Sfx (as I stop off at Anne Kennedy's house)
Triumph 2000 1970 FK8344 steams   and crackles
cooling off   drip   drip   of joyous frost
melting from *hoheria* and ti ngahere.
Knock at door.
No answer.
Leave it in the letter-box.
At the other end of Norfolk St, Peter Brunt
is looking for a park.
Honk but he doesn't hear.
Fish Shop Gallery to the left in Ponsonby Rd.
Last night the Elam students' print
exhibition, Anna's etching titled *Table Talk*
(a hen on a table) and Helen's *Night Travels* (a monoprint) —
Night Travels or Night *Travels*?
Either/both, she said.
Night *Shift* or *Night* Shift?
A question I ask myself.
Hard to say now, hard to say
so long ago, long ago and, and
far away, you said then those 'Night Shift Poems'
sounded like Frank O'Hara. They were meant to.
But I don't stop off in Tole St to
tell you so even though I'm driving that way.
Nor stop to tell you at Alexis Hunter's opening
Ngahuia invoked the 'verdant paths of Grafton'.
Somehow it never seems to be the right day
for nostalgia.
There's only one way to get about —
visiting people you don't know who aren't there
or not knocking on old friends' doors.
Only one way of getting it all down —
in the wrong order.
Say this is Tuesday.   9.00 a.m.
Blood on hands. Heart aflutter.

No place to go but merge
with the writing on the wall
Sell Treasury
Trick Or Treaty
Be My Valentine
melting those lines in the hot pan of lyric desire
23 years ago yesterday
on the still face of the turning earth
on Fire Island
you took simply the next step when what's taking
the next step when you have already taken the last?
You might have enjoyed it here
though some of the fizz has leaked from the cylinder
and the downbeat falls every hour
there's still a day ahead
in Auckland with the temperature rising
you'd still be only 63
and getting across town is a tempestuous pleasure
still young at heart/slim but mature in mind
wearing the tight trousers of spent purpose and
hopeless love
and foolish enough to go looking for it again
feeling your way forward
into that feeling
and loving the way that feels

Script
(for Meyerhold 1874-1940)

Open with rare footage from Centennial Exhibition.
Include shots of cameras of newly-formed
National Film Unit. Track back to c.u. art deco curve
of handrail. L.s. of four Russian puppeteers setting up
between Forestry and Fisheries.
Potted conifers. Face in camera. A cabotin.
V/O: 'Make no mistake about it,
the thing that you will see happening
tonight is really happening this very night!'

Exhibition Hall almost empty. Few late stragglers
straggle. Silhouette shapes turn in audience.
Shot of Pierrot marionette on stick dangling.
Cabotin speaks: 'Today is February 2nd 1940!
Our play takes place in a tiny flat in Moscow.
It is midwinter.'
Lights flicker as if a shoulder leant on the switch.
A figure from the sinister side, KGB hat and coat,
sited shooting home movie in background.

C.u. on puppet booth.
Spiderish Pierrot and pale scythe-like Columbine
are cooking dinner. One pot. One ring.
Reminiscing of the old days.
He: 'Do you not understand the play in which
ours will not be the final role?'
She: 'Role.' Cabotin: 'Gentlemen! Our poor friend
has been driven mad by fear. He never thought about
what we were preparing for all our lives . . .

also the quality of the celluloid. This footage
was shot in 1906.'
A knock at the door.
Talk of the old days is stuffed in a drawer.
Znaida, his little Columbine, crosses the room.
Opens the door. And there are one two three four
murderous Harlequins sucking acid drops.

L.s. through exit doors. To Rongotai beyond.
Salt scattered to sea music on Miramar rooftop tin.

Vesvolod Emelivich Pierrot Meyerhold: 'You
are making a mistake. This is Columbine. This
is my bride.'
First Man: 'You're out of your mind.
All evening we have waited for an event.
At last it has occurred. She's come to us,
this quiet deliverer. Death has visited us.'
VEPM: 'I don't listen to fairy tales.
I'm a simple man. You won't fool me.'

A puppet of a car is guided in across
the polished linoleum. The men fit Vesvolod
in the back seat between their shoulders.
The custodians flick the lights a last time.
Shot of puppeteers packing Columbine
in her box behind the booth. Documentary
light. Feet that squeak. The cabotin's face
with its grey eyes, white cheeks, and sad beak
on shambling frame in puffed-up satin:

'The Author wanted to remind you
he wrote a thoroughly realistic play.
That he does not admit any legends,
any such vulgarities!'
L.s. of tiny car leaving Hall of Progress.
Custodians locking up.
Puppeteers struggling through wind with flats and curtains.
Thinness of bodies.
Light, air, night and wind. And paper.

Treating of Why Ten Eyes Weep

I have studied the science of goodbyes
— Mandelshtam

When you received your goodbye
(*sotto voce*, knife at the throat)
you became an umbrella tinted in
where the face used to be, part
of a woman's skirt, erasure
in a bath of fixer (you were cut
down so softly with a ponytail
for a scythe). You were arranged
round your absence, you became
a nation reduced to single

exhibition with art deco curves,
a theatre in permanent rehearsal
whose first night never arrived.
The mural is by Mr F. Coventry
and New Zealand's own empire
is on display: Niue, Samoa,
the Cooks, gripped in that
1940 handshake, Micky Savage
and the tamatoa surrounded by
the armies of potted conifers.

Vsevolod Emelivich Meyerhold
nobody missed you here. Znaida's
mutilated body was not reported.
Your recantation remained recusant.
A cabotin without an acid drop.
We were arranging our own harlequinade,
thanks. The only thing we have in
common is our photos too look doctored now.
That's Chekhov at the back. And Gorky.

The Thirty-Six Dramatic Situations

1
I asked him by looking at him.
I asked him by taking off my shoes.

By dancing that dance.
Supplicating my neck.

2
She took me out of myself.
I stood in the shadow of a tree,
a path of steps.
A taxi drew up.
It backed fatally far,
its wheels hung over the concrete edge,
chassis on concrete.
No way out.

3
Delivered like a baby
he fled the city in an aeroplane
but she followed him.
Agreeing to meet at the end of the wharf.
Lots of yachts locked
in docks.

4
If the son found out.
If the daughter found out.
Electrifying and arresting.
They sit like snakes
in the furious room.
Her drugged body breathes through the wall.

5
She wakes up.
Leaves the house.
Footsteps.
Speeds up.
A corner.
Shoplight.
Take a taxi.
Cannot be followed.
To his door.

6
Sell sell sell.
Everything.
Every last brick.
Rock bottom embraces.
At the airport, a line of well-known faces.
Disaster.

7
Circumstances made her go back to him.
Let him wait as long as he envisages.

He let the pale ghost of trepidation
muddy his doorstep.

He ate shit
because they asked him to.

In a small room full of books
with no desire to read.

8
Gagging on words,
money revolts you,
stings skin where it touches,
sunlight burns, darkness
eats your mind,
your children look straight ahead,
you flounder.

9
So begin with a project.
Arrange date, mood, escapade.
Delete fear.
Behave like a different person.
Prance around with your life
in your hands.

10
And then one night he steals you.
There on the back seat
feeling the maniacal swerves of his driving
heave your body here and there
the cochleas swung in a scream of imbalance,
he takes you to that place
he once talked about:
everything is neatly arranged:
the tins, the skins, the bars,
the beans.

11
The phone calls came first.
Then signs: things turned,
objects displaced,
a face at a window, no
one outside.

12
Obtaining to what, whom?
Obtaining whom, what for what, whom?
Obtaining power over others.
A money-back course.

13
Brother against brother
mother against son
wife against husband
hoar frost
a withered branch
a hint of insanity

a marriage of unspeakable degradation.
Your last hope.

14
Both wanted her,
met in the café to discuss
possible ways of sharing,
alternations,
simultaneities,
exclusions,
perversions,
dimensions of trade.
A house of bonded free men.

15
Simplicity is the most attractive feature.
You hold it.
Draw back.
As he opens the door.
Push past.
She's there.
You smile as planned.
He follows you in.
You turn.
He stops in the doorway.
And then you plunge it in.
In and up.
Under the ribs and turn it, curl it,
till the heart ruptures
on your spit.
Not for her.
Murderous adultery.

16
He'd never felt saner.
Never had his stocks floated with such buoyancy.
Never before the energy.
The sheer dream of living
lived out
openly

fearlessly.
And always the verge of choking.

17
A sunny afternoon.
In his office, working.
That faint knock, the
fatal imprudence.
After all he'd been through
to put himself through more.
Rogered by his own spectacle.

18
He stole for her.
Bent his neck for her to bite.
Wept coins on her garlic hair.
Gifted shares in a flood of love.
Lent his book of taxi chits,
queued in banks for time
to drop its rain of skin.
They flew everywhere,
did everything.
And still no one seemed to know
what was going on between them.
The tension in the auditorium
was palpable as a pin.

19
A simple accident.
Late at night.
Together in the car.
Laughing.
A brother steps to the kerb
and doesn't look.
It's the evasive action you take
which kills.

20
So give up everything,
start again.

Make sure no one's on your side.
Proceed to demolish any hope of gain.
Pack your batteries with a pure
burning fuel.
Execrate promise.

21
And for her children's sake
she came back to the gothic *arrangement*.
Coinage
in a bad joke.

22
A house full of beds.
Beds full of bodies.
Bodies full of blood.
The full-on classical
cash-flow crisis.

23
He hung on to her chances.
He wouldn't stop nagging her doubts.
He made her pay with feelings.
She had to dig a pit for him.

24
Hall of doors,
dish of whores —
stew it!
Roger and out.

The littler man wants
the bigger man's wife
and the bigger man wants
a quieter life.

Harmonics.
Whore-manics.
The wife wants a bite
of the country cooking.

25
So when it happens,
late in the afternoon,
upstairs with the TV on,
only an hour before he returns
from the meeting
they wonder why they had
waited so long.

26
Rouge her.
Crimes of love.

27
He sold his father's story
to the newspapers.
Twenty, thirty,
years ago.

Still telling that story,
shoulder on the jukebox,
blankness in his eyes.

28
The transport system
money
the wind
a hill
sleepiness
inhibition
delay
satisfaction
who gets up to make breakfast
for who —
obstacles to love.

29
An enemy loved.
A friend reviled.
A revelation dismayed.
A smile disrobed.

30
Years casting round for a subject
big enough for his ego.
Bought, did up, and sold
five houses in one year.
Still his father's words
nibbled his desires.
Her ankles and the arches
of her feet
made him lurch with pleasure.
His whole reason.

31
Free to choose
you chose wrongly.
Resorting to blasphemy
you heard your own lack of conviction.
Forgiveness
begged too late.
Contrition no salve.
Cacoethes vivendi.
Whore to your own ambition
you took no pleasure in it.
Worship a numbness.

32
She wanted him to
so she could hate him
for it.
Downstage left, eyes
just over the heads
of the audience
the full wind
of passion
misplaced.

33
The taxi's wheels spinning in the air.

34
A signal of pain
carried over a great distance
to reassure a loved one
the nights will grow warmer.

35
Prodigious feasting
in mock-marble halls.
Tales of reconciled swine.

36
And the one who never came back.
Delayed. Deleted. Dilated.
Dutchman.
The seven seas.
And for ever.
The last third of the semiosis
suspended indefinitely.

Notes

Road Movie Canto Rangatihi upoko i takaia ki te akatea — Rangatihi's head was bound with akatea.

After being ambushed, Rangatihi took the small, creeping white rata vine (akatea) and bound up his split skull with it, rallied his companions, and won the fight. The moral is, don't give up. I learnt this whakatauki on the slopes of Pirongia but I do not know if it is local to that region. Akatea is *Metrosideros albiflora*, the white-flowered *Metrosideros*, from *metra*, womb, matrix or heartwood, and *sideron*, iron.

Hirsute Canine Narrative The words '. . . pieces of fossilized gum . . . moa crop . . ./of jasper . . . oven stones . . . shale spills . . . middens . . .' are all from Kendrick Smithyman's poem 'Tomarata'.

Pnigos Pnigos: literally 'a choke'. In Greek comedy it refers to a long passage which should be chanted in one breath for comic effect. The whole of the poem 'Pnigos' in one breath would defeat anyone; but one breath per stanza is fun. Pnigos was not the name of the island in the poem. The island was, in fact, Waiheke.

Script On December 30th 1906 Meyerhold staged Alexander Blok's play *The Fairground Booth* or *The Puppet Booth*. Meyerhold took the role of Pierrot in the production. He later wrote an important essay which he titled 'The Fairground Booth' and which contained his ideas about a new theatre. I am grateful to Brian Boyd for translating Blok's play for me, and some of the lines which the characters speak in the poem 'Script' are from his translation. Brian is not responsible for my manipulation of the play into the poem. 'Treating of Why Ten Eyes Weep' makes use of a Russian pun — the coincidence of the words 'scythe' and 'ponytail' — drawn from the same play. Meyerhold was murdered by the state in February 1940 apparently for refusing to recant his ideas about theatre.